It's about time

Malcolm Cooke

But if in your thought you must measure time into seasons, let each season encircle all the other seasons, And let today embrace the past with remembrance and the future with longing.

Kahil Gibran - The Prophet

For my dear friend Lorraine with much love

Malcolm

Contents

Beginnings

We met and didn't notice the meeting.
It began like that.
An old, old story waiting to be retold
and in the telling I learnt your name.
And when, casual, you asked me mine,
I told you shyly. As though confessing.
Oh, I was, I was.
And if I'm asked where it all began,
I will say that moment then,
in that second of unknowing,
before the coming of the Judas kiss.

Waiting

My hands move,
empty gestures.
My mouth talks,
empty words.
My eyes see,
empty spaces.
I am not here.

The clock moves,
not enough.
The coffee pours,
not yours.
The phone rings,
not you.
You are not here.

I've been sitting,
I've been counting heartbeats,
counting the breath.
The hours falling away slowly.
I am sitting waiting.
There should be more beats,
more beats and less breath.
It's taking too long
this waiting for you.

Love poem

Tongue touch tells of love,
snaking its word into your mouth,
searching the echo of your tongue,
tasting the confirmation.
Teeth glide hallmarks of love,
on necks and shoulders and breasts,
I bite gentle savage
and your skin sets your teeth
in motion.
Nips of love sing electric chills
spine bend straight shock,
breaths twine together
tighter than our legs,
looser than our hands.
From fingers come sea
crashing waves moulding bones
searching skin, that was not before
love unfolding, and then the warm.
Oh the touch the singing dance
the burning wet wanting -
I want - you want.
O the want.
The fingernail sculpts
tracks and highways,
flagging new byways.
Fingertip suck
of lips and love,
the clinging spasms of joy
in the melt and the coming
O love - love O
the strangled cry.

Woman

Oh Woman,
You cast your soul like a net ,
forever searching through the ebb and the flow
for the man, to bring you safe to shore,
to where you were before.

Oh Woman,
do you take this man,
this fisher of memories,
this weaver of dreams?
Then gird him with your mantle of power,
take refuge in his arms
and believe
this is the man.

Ah Woman,
grey are your uncried tears
and silent your grieving heart
and in a whisper of mourning,
you offer up holy prayers.
Oh heavenly Father,
This was a man of flesh
sent to cut me loose,
and now I am adrift
and drifting.
He was a sculptor of tears,
a passing wave
caught upon the reef of desire
and illusion.
It was a moment of madness
and this is not the man.

4

Oh child,
still begging forgiveness,
still searching for a truth
that never was.
Trapped in your womanhood,
a private darkness,
betrayed and oh so broken
you sob to the man who slipped under
 - and away -
Oh Daddy, Daddy. Why?
And in your ageless grief
you blame the man
for who he is not - Oh woman.

Back to Back

You lie with your back facing
my back. I lie listening.
No sleep surf tonight.
Sometimes a sob, clutched back tight,
more often the snake still silence
coiled around you.

We have known this night before.
We have breathed the breath,
tasted the salt sour
uneasy gap sprawled between us.
No skin warm tangle of arms,
legs to bind us close.
Not tonight.

So many words that could have been,
and those that shouldn't
have spilled
Past the thought and the tongue
To thicken the darkness.

I lie confused, lost in guilt,
armed with blame. Still do not,
do not know how to move,
move blackness,
move you.
Once I would have been brave.

I dare my fingers to your back, praying
that this night I be the Messiah.
But your skin speaks in tongues -
Casting out demons.
You need nothing. You want nothing.
You are wrapped
behind blankets, beyond solace.

Tonight you wear your shroud,
and I miss your warmth.
I lie listening.
I hear only your sleep song
murmuring, as we lie back to back.

Love in the Shadows

Today, Inshalla,
your finger tips will pause as you pass.
A kiss of air on my shoulder,
hidden to the world.
An empty breeze of no consequence.

I, in turn, will breathe.

Breathe and burn.
For I am undone in a tsunami of fire.
Branded with your love, made holy,
I will breathe for both of us.
A breath of aching desire, a flare
of hope in darkness
showing nothing.
Muffled in modesty, my longing stands mute.

Your silence,
an emptiness tongued with hidden tears
A banquet without guests,
Binds me with promises, begs patience.
Leaves me wanting.
In the wake of your shadow's shadow
I will measure out the arrival of absence;
counting beats, weighing your touch,
rehearsing in scenes without colour,
without sound, how we shall next meet.

On that day,
I shall raise my eyes
in defiance.
Unveil
the landscape of my soul.
Reveal the future from the past.
On that day,
I will wait for the warm embrace of your words.

And today, Inshalla,
Will you tarry, brush against my arm?
Once, maybe twice?
Will the morse code of your heart
Break out, liberate us both?
Or will we take solace,
Give thanks, silent prayers
that we met in recognition?

I have the scraps,
scooped, scavenged from our days,
burnished with love and memory.
I live gladly
Knowing one day,
One day my fingers will trace your face,
And your lips will kiss my palm.
One day.
Inshalla.

Heart break

Even the warm wish of a razor,
that glides like the loving kiss
of a long lost friend,
cutting through time and wrists and arteries
cannot bring the circle full round.

And in the deathly pale
of this deathless realm,
with hearts stripped naked
of words and time,
the ghosts of love burnt out
come together once more.

Ah - a touch of raw honesty,
a welcome cut,
sharper than the knife that slicks
and sings in the pulsing wound.

And from the ashes of passions spent
comes the burning ache,
and each throb brings me closer,
yet takes me further.

And in the dimming of the night
the pain in my heart grows brighter,
and in the quiet time
before the coming of the light,
before the day begins
before the birds start their chant,
in that unmoving no-time
before the last drop has seeped away,
my heart beats - once - twice
your name - always your name
and beats no more.

Ghost

I thought you had long gone,
at least that was what you wanted,
and I tried, oh how I tried
to forget.
And yet..
in the empty silences
I hear your whisper still.
I feel your soft touch,
a finger to the lips curved in air,
mouthed in music,
is that you there?
And when my eyes close
I see your breath in
the colour of the sky,
shimmering,
wrapping me round,
and I'm sure, oh so sure,
I hold you still.
If I could undo all of our words,
remove the echoes from the walls,
dismantle our hours from the days,
our joys from the nights.

If I could do this and more,
then you could leave.
But you have claimed the minutes,
each and every one,
and in all I do
you haunt me still.

Moment of acceptance

There was
No heavenly fanfare
No shift in the orbits of sun and moon
No sudden eclipse, day was day, night still night
No hail or brimstone
No movement of the earth
No darkening of the light
No change in the wind
No trembling hands
No spilling of coffee
No sharp intake of breath
No shedding of tears
No knowing looks or regrets
No recriminations
No farewells
No random heartbeats
No what ifs or buts
No maybes to hang on to
No signs for the world to see.

There was simply
A breathing in, a letting go.
And life moved on.

Revelations

Tonight I'm drunk from watching clouds
Seeing the slip slap of time dipping away
The horizon draining pink to grey

Soothed by the trickle chink of words on glass,
the back basking honeysuckle warmth,
I shed the cloak of my day, let it slide,
welcome the earth breath beat inside.
I sink. I float. I breathe. I drown. I forget.
I am
lost
in your embrace like the song of a bird
pinned to the sky.
Tracing the soft curve of sweet surrender,
familiar, old as orbiting stars, we reach out.
A glance of fingers exposes
knowing hands that have loved
in the vapours of dreams, or forgotten lives,
unravelling memories

We waltz the trees, hills, the greens and golds,
shape shift our bones to rock and stone,
swirl the rivers and stream in blood,
drift forever on tides that never turn.
Dust and time wrapped in gossamer voices,
waiting to be made flesh, searching for signs.
The world moves, from dark to light
to dark we tumble
our edges blur, shadows and shades rise,
and we
are fading, falling apart.

Tonight I'm drunk from portents,
omens scattered around my days.
Your voice, I heard it already old in my heart,
ancient as oak. Maybe.
There is nothing, not this night, not this round.
Some other world carved from possibilities
has slipped quietly away.

Tonight I'm drunk from watching clouds,
dreaming of tomorrows that never come.

Sacrifice

Today I am the dying man
sacrificed to the larger plan.
Still beating out the sea voice flamenco
from which the Word was born,
the still bleeding heart
is torn ragged from the breast,
and on an altar of wind and waves
is carved in sacrificial rite
by a hand mightier than the breath
in my lungs.

Cast into the blackness
a lonely incantation.
One more flickering soul
scattered with the dead
and the Word which was
is no more.

Today I am the living child
conceived in the spume of chaos
nurtured in the darkening light
until the heart burning virgin white
takes frail flesh and bones,
calls upon the one voice
for release.

And in the echo of the silence
the body was consumed by fire.
And now I am the seven seas,
the four winds, heaven and earth,
sky and water,
more than this fragile shell,
yet less than I seem.
I am the word.

Sunsets

1.
Eventide,
the outward breath fading,
slipping away with style,
into the falling melt of sun and sea
and looking back,
and beyond,
all is as it was
and meant to be.

2.
Your last whisper -
Come to the sea,
Dip your hands in my soul,
and if I slip through and away, forgive me.
Can you – would you do that?
Beneath the sky I will be brine blessed ,
twice blessed with your love,
and you will taste the sweet tang
left on your fingers.
And when you are ready
come back to the sea.

Driftwood

Caught by a watery hand,
carried I know not where,
nor care,
through currents and tides,
wind and stars,
my edges licked smooth by sea-salt caresses
my heart bleached white,
purified
a child of sun and moon.
Caught in the hand of a hand
I am driftwood.

Dreaming of dragons

Lift the silken veil. Softly.
From my days.
Slowly, like defusing a lover,
open the dream,
ease the pennies from my eyes,
an offering of my hours.
A small price, gladly paid
for dreaming of dragons.

Leaf fall

I watch a leaf fall.
In still air.
Crisped edges sharp in russet light,
roll and tumble like a kitten at play.
In air still,
it draws in
the breath of the world,
pauses,
balances
for a single moment,
holding
the weight of all that has ever been.
Oh
A sigh, a lament, a slipping away,
a fall from grace.
A see-saw cut through thinning space
where Angels take time,
time to wonder
at beginnings and endings
and falling leaves,
and wonder….
at what remains.
Empty, breathless air
touched
by the memory of a homecoming,
waiting for a breeze.

March

It was warm,
much warmer than we'd hoped,
and we walked,
not far but much further than we thought
and we touched in the coffee spice air,
not a lot, but enough.
It was warm,
much warmer than people saw.

Moments

The steps of our lives dance a secret waltz,
time travel together in mystery, yours mingled
with mine from long before I was knowing.
There is beauty in the choreography of chance,
of how we get from there to here,
then to now; to arrive together,
to where we've always been headed;
A convergence of choices, moments unfolding
and folding
one into the other like waves upon the shore,
a choir of notes creating a song we've not yet heard
or rehearsed.
.

Sepia

Two people caught within a sepia frame;
The opening paragraph of a new life
already run its course, her maiden name
traded on the altar for someone's wife

Hand in arm you stand, a lover's caress,
shy like breath. With forget-me-not garland -
blue notes, which will fall limp like your dress,
the scattered ruins of a one night stand.

Where now your posy, double edged sweet peas?
Did they wither slowly, the colours fade?
Or dried and lost with other memories?
Or was love's measure with plucked petals weighed?

Liver spot stained, your hand in hers, more frail
than the weight of years, they tell the true tale.

For lovers of preposterous beauty

What is it catches you unaware,
steals your breath? Leaves your words
hung without form. Once you were blind
now you see for the first time -
nothing new

Light furrowed angles of blue
green and gold rolling away,
The season of bales and harvest
wrapping round touching your blood,
the sharp intensity cutting through
binding you in communion

And then comes the flood,
rushing in, taking you down.
The memories of all you have loved -
a touch,
a kiss,
the sound of a voice,
the smell of a flower,
holding your child's hand.

Your heart unfolds,reaches out
for the love still to come
and you are lost to the world

And in the face of such beauty
you summon the word
Preposterous

Kith and Kin

I carry kith and kin upon my back,
a gift bag of ghosts,
memories loosely tied with tendrils
of time stolen from mud and stone,
places called home,
blood and bone collected
from wherever I am touched;
offerings for the taking
when one collects alms.

Each day my bowl is filled :

A boy and girl strolling,
proclaiming to the world
to which they are blind,
their hand in hand gently holding
the force of first love everlasting.
And I am minded to say
one day, someone,
will love you as I do now -
without expectation, for who you are.
My love will travel your journey
unannounced by your side, to give hope
when your hands unclasp.

An old woman,
gnarled and bent leaning forever forward
like a single moor wracked hawthorn,
raises her head, sagely straw protected.
With a smiling 'Bon appetit', she captures us,
two tourists walking in sunshine, eating ice-cream,
adding an alm to her eclectic collection,
to share and savour on a damp winters evening.
Then she is gone
and we are lifted higher into her sun.

In a world shaped by small inconsequences,
what matters blood? it has no prerogative
to stake a claim upon the heart,
to pull rank because of thickness.
The shared shreds of dna
rooted in some ancient rutting
unravel at the drop of a word
or a slight of look, or simple neglect
and blood runs cold.

Give me honest water, the common kind
that sloshes round in the day to day,
to anoint and bathe the sinews
of who we are,
and every word, every touch are but hints
of the currents which bind.

Night Skies

A clear winter's eve
walking with my father,
a child still, asking questions.
And he valiant
told all there was to know
as only fathers can.
Start with an apple
green like the earth,
a moon bright marble
going round and round.
Hold them in your hand
and spin arms outstretched.
You are night and day,
seasons that come and go
A dancing sun,
magnificent
yet still nought but a speck
against the blackness.

That was then.

And now

I am a grandfather
waiting out my winter,
a novice still.
And this night canvas
awakens old man thoughts.
My dad's voice,
a whisper in time,
still cannot answer why.
I have to go to ground,
anchor my soul to rock and root,
against the swell and pull.
Count them one by one, on and on,
from beginning to end,
awe stippled flecks of light
shimmering on the edge of sight.

Each an angel, or wish, or what you will -
forged from time, from tears, promises.
Or a child spinning the future,
holding my hand,
touching my heart.

The Greening

After a troubled and restless winter
I heard the breath of a lover waking,
long weeks waiting, whispered
on the wind.
She'd stirred, turned her face,
and sun-kissed hinted
of desire.
Offered
to a morning mist her first flush,
her melting shush of rose grey
stencilled in lime green filigree.
I felt her fluid caress
quickening
heartbeats,
calling
sap to bone,
earth to blood,
bird to song.
me to her.

After a long and sleepless night
waiting for the world to turn,
I walked the sun to greet her.
She wore
a simple verdant gown,
draped across the muted land,
star pierced with blackthorn white.
A bride to be, an age old pact -
With my body I thee wed.

Bent to her love, fierce and driven,
the wedding dress undone.
She claimed me, laid me open,
uncovered my eyes, to witness,
to worship her greening

World Events

Today the world turned,
a voice was raised. Let it go.
Let go. Let it be.

A weight of snow upon the stave,
frost channelled through veins
one crystal at a time.

This is how the world ends

Wonder at a fluttering star
framed cold by broken glass.
Look to the sea, to the night,
remember a dream of home,
a chill to the bone.

This is how the world ends.

A kiss left hanging, love spurned,
one more heart draped in rain,
drowning.

This is how the world ends.

A last breath, clinging to lips in prayer,
searching for a second wind
enough to fill a sail, to raise a shout.

Is this how the world ends?

The compact chosen to travel blind,
to live the life uncharted,
a twisted path obscured by clouds;
from worlds within worlds
to carve a world without end.

That is how it all begins.

Yawn and wipe the sleep away
Brush the snow from the stoop
scrape the ice from the screen
small steps along the day.
Welcome the postman, start the car,
an old road transformed anew
black ice sharpened eyes.
Fingers curled wary tight
distance measured in heartbeats,
a journey within a journey.
The warmth of arriving
face to face with a stranger
yet to be a lover.

Today the world turned.
This is how it works

Surrounded by Mountains

A holiday in Scotland,
surrounded by mountains
A place of unwinding in a world unbinding.

Once, it might have been Sarajevo,
a cauldron fed by passions, religions
drip dripped through pent up centuries

Would I have understood the sharp tongues
propping a failed wedding,
the trail of bad blood sketching history,

Now, yet more ailing marriages;
pins in a map on a wall, labelled
with a common cause.
Rooted in time and nonsense,
burdened with belief.
Divorce is not enough for them,
how could it be?
Cleansing is required,
a purgative, an emetic to be applied,
a burning out of sects and towns.

The scent of suffering carries on the wind,
raking up desire, to avenge.
I want to kill.

And if I kill,
by proxy or otherwise,
whose son will it be?
Who will taste the fleeting
stab of justice?
Who will say a job well done?
Who will bind me to their cause?

And if I kill,
by claiming the might of right,
will it ease grief? Soothe sorrows?
Appease your anger?
Give you back your home,
your father, your mother, your child?
Will it?
Will it be forgiven more
than if I do nothing,
if I refuse to be a groom
at another blood wedding?

I sit here, surrounded by mountains,
where clan once fought clan,
where the dead are long rested.
A holy day,
a day for making peace with myself.
And I'm fighting for an uneasy truce,
for somewhere to begin.

The Plimsoll Line

Twenty four caskets óf white
on white drifts of mourning.

Are you sleeping heart?

Shores awash with bodies,
a cumulus of unknown faces,
their stories stolen, hidden in waves,
buried as numbers in a news report.
Did their clamour for life
not wake you?

Are you sleeping hurt,
maybe moved to murmur,
wondering where love has fled.
Dust and blood, ochre, red,
marooned in silver gilt
whispering here, here.

Are you listening heart?
The voices have gone,
cast off
one by one,
And in the silence do you yet hear
their call?

Are you still asleep heart?
Look.
A child's plimsoll, washed clean
of its previous life,
lifts and rolls, pirouettes,
destitute on the water's edge;
A solo dance without a dancer,
a script with the wrong line.

Are you mute heart?
Twenty four caskets of white
on white drifts of mourning
await a voice.

How to cross safely

Be full of care, my children
when crossing the road,
for frail flesh is no match
when head on with steel.
Choose where you can see
your future clear
into the distance.
Listen, for time unfolding,
forget your past and your return.
Simply walk.
I will be here for you.
Waiting.

Beware, my children,
of crossing open spaces,
where a bullet can consume
the unwary heart.
Better to slide along walls,
hug shadows to your skin,
be invisible to prying eyes.
Pick your path,
each step a revelation of your fate,
every footfall a benediction
for others to follow.
Shroud your light in darkness,
a keepsake to unveil on your return.
Come safely, relieve the anguish
of my waiting.

Twilight

Travelling the twilight.
A day dying in the last post
of a lone blackbird;
distance dimmed, colours gone.
Flit of bat, from the corner
of an eye, a shadow breath.
I stand time leached,
poised at the gate
of death and rebirth.
Alive and ready.

All that I am

I am the colour of skin,
the shape of the nose,
the slant of an eye,
the lip of a strange tongue,
the forbidden embrace.
I am the difference.
I am your ignorance
and fear.

I am the creed, the spiller of faith,
the evangelist, the converter.
I am the burka, the crucifix,
the little Red book,
the party manifesto.
The one truth.
A rock for a hollow man
to fall through.

I am the man, breaker of bones.
I am the man, setter of traps.
I am the man, violator.
I am the man, finger on the trigger
purveyor of war,
killer.
I am the man afraid of love.

I am your shadow face
the blind sided twin stalking your sleep,
walking your days.
Skirting darkness and light, I am
the echo behind, an emptiness within.
I am curse and cure,
a loyal companion holding court
on the edge of your sight.
I am the waiting witness
of becoming.
Without you, I am
Nothing.

Such a day

Was it a day such as this
when first we kissed?
Was it a day such as this
when first we touched?
Was it a day such as this
when first we met?
Was it a day such as this
when it all began?
Oh what a day this day is.

Encounters

When I turn to see
your sleeping hair upon the pillow,
flecks of silver grey
creeping through the dark, or maybe
when I await your coming into a room
and you appear, or the passing touch
of fingers on my shoulder, or the tide
of your body coming home.
When you sit across with coffee talking
of the commonplace and I watch your mouth,
or your profile caught sideways by the sun
like the first time.
When you are near,
all words become undone, fall apart
and I am lost - again.

The love song of Mr Cafferty

Mr Cafferty, old and rickety,
had to walk with a stickety
tippety tap sort of stick.
Every night on the stroke of eight
he went to his garden gate,
not fast nor slow but just so
tappety tip tap tap straight.
There loud and clear, he'd call
for all to hear : oh pretty prettily,
it's time to rest, to leave the slink
and the slide. No more chasing birds
or stalking spiders, so inside
velvet pink padded paws
gently glide your claws.
And as I snuggle to the TV,
happily slurping tea,
Come curl on my knee -
let me ruffle through
your flibberty, flabberty fur
to hunt the rumbly rumble purr.

I have Facebook

I have Facebook,
thin links for friends,
thinner than blood,
thinner than water,
even thinner than air itself.
Round robin snowflakes of trivia,
measures of shared intimacy
meaning what exactly?
I strive to be hidden, mute,
and yet you made the effort,
still felt it necessary, managed to bypass
the strictures of time, thirty years
blossoming as a hashtag
slipping away without a word.
Or a like.

I do not remember

I do not
remember the words left unsaid, hovering like gadflies
around goodbye
I do not remember how I slept into a dream where you
    walked,
arm in arm, shoulder to cry on, saying remember when

I don't
remember the house where we lived, grand it seemed,
with a coal cellar. And a parlour. I do not remember the
    times
I lay there watching the day fade, waiting for the
    lamplighter.
I do, I do not remember how I grew in that house.

I do not remember picking the mint for the sauce,
watching the chop chop of the knife curving through
    green leaves,
a trail of juice upon the board, the mix of sugar and
    vinegar.

I don't remember many flowers in the yard, lupins
and red hot pokers near the mangle.
I don't remember why you didn't let go while I turned
and turned
the handle, feeding your finger to the rollers.
Red hot rollers.

I do not remember the times between waking and
    sleeping,
nor the waking into days of watching rare vapour trails

dissolve, fading back to blue.
I do not remember the dying of the days, warm summer
    evenings
lying abed, nor the injustice of kids still out on the street
    below
I do not remember the wheeling murmurations spilling
across my window, harbingers of the night.

I do
not remember, how could I, the tightropes walked,
the eddies of lives swirling, colliding one with the other.
You and you and you and you.
I do not remember how you managed the helm,
holding true to some unknown destination
I do not remember you growing old

I don't remember so very much.

You are missed

In the deep deep dark, in the depths
of a bird's lament
you are missed.
I turn, I turn
In this long, long night of winter's repair
I turn, I yearn for you not there
Missing, missed.

We have arrived at the space,
the empty hole after a full stop. The full
stop
Of a well worded sentence,
where well lived words come to rest.
And come the morning all words have fled,
we are now unfinished.
Without your words I have nothing.
You are missed.

I have discovered the void, aching
aching to be filled.
Hoar breath upon skin ashen white
has stolen my centre. I am gone to the world,
rudderless, my pole star blinded.
If I knew where, I would follow; for nothing remains.
We are missing and missed.

The pulse of the world, paused between beats,
waits no more, the sanctus sung
alchemy begins.
Hallowed light spills and seeps
to fill the valley, to touch and kiss the earth,

to anoint where you walked,
and your work springs forth for all to see.
But not for you.
Not this time.
I want to see your face light up again,
crinkle knowingly as you say "See."
I imagine your fingers deep in the soil,
a labour of love.
You are missed, missed, missed.

Another solstice, still seeking solace.
Nights are short and sleepless.
In the half light my hand grasps
at emptiness, heavy laden crushing my heart.
You are missed.
You have taken my voice, the one I shared with you,
and you alone,
our plans, our little secrets
peppered across the pillows
all gone.
Sometimes in dreams we meet,
you speak and I tremble at your words
'You are missed.
Be strong, go on.'

The cashmere shawl warmth of a summer evening
wraps me round softly.
I sit out, as we once did, upon our bench,
The lolling dogs at my feet, the wall's heat
attempting to hint of past glories.
I look out across our valley,

49

find I am blind, my vision tainted.
I no longer see as I did.
Your memory blocks my view.
I now see with your eyes
clearer than with my own.
And I feel you ever present
and yet
you are missed
and not missed.

Nature notes

This is a book.
Look child,
this is a tree.
See honeyed chocolate wood, smooth
flowing through trunk and branches,
A candelabra wearing a hair snood of mint green leaves,
Each taken from the master leaf in the artist's eye.
Trunk, branch and leaf; brown and green
The untruth by which all trees are known.

This too is a book,
a guide to the truth of trees
as found in the British Isles.
Each page proclaims: I am born of wood, out of tree,
my history bleached white, made ready
for the lie of a likeness of my kin.
From this taxonomy of fine indian ink line,
loose leaf bound with words, circumnavigated
by averages of height and breadth
a name can be conjured,
no more substantial than the rustle
of paper.
Listen.
Here is oak.
Here is yew.
Ash, willow, beech and birch.
They are but whispers, no more solid
than psalms at vespers.

Here is truth.
You must forget all you know,

51

or believe to be true.
I am tree.
Forever upstretched to pray,
sway and pray, unceasing without rest,
a wind song to heaven.
Feet corralled at birth, earth cosseted;
rooted to time, to the pin prick
of my death, a whole life bound
to contemplation, the solitude
of a monk.

I am tree.
I travel time, enduring.
I see the sun rise, I see the sun set,
The seasons which mould my heart
come and go.
I have seen your fleetness of foot,
the quickness of spirit flaring
full of importance, looking to make a mark,
but you are like the breeze
skipping over the world.
You are here
and then you are gone;
A sometime sparkle of light.

I am tree
Come stand with me.
Be still, reach your arms round
anchor your fingers,
Let my corrugations scent your fingerprints.

Come closer, trunk to trunk.
Turn your head, lay your cheek like a lover
against my body, close your eyes,
tune the antennae of your palms
ready to receive communion.
I will offer you the weight of my history,
the measure of my spirit,
the song of the earth which runs
through my core.
I will sing to your heart a hymn like no other.
Then you will know me.
I am tree.

Your Turn

Coming ready or not.

Not the first, certainly not the last.
Like migrating birds following forgotten routes
chosen long ago,
who understand when they arrive
of the need to fly.

And from this vantage point of a laggard,
what can be said?
One would not wait, would not swim.
Let the waves wash her sin.
Another.
Grasping for the grace of tomorrows,
for time enough to dream,
knew before the moment of knowing -
his course was true.
And others. They came, went, left traces
in memories and secret places.

The scent of a life lingering.
Each dawn fainter than the last,
until the stories are gone,
faces orphaned in sepia photos.
Oh how they fade, always fade
these lives without history.

But you, you my friend, have cut me loose,
not by any choice we recognise or would choose.
My heart weeps days and hours, time itself drained dry
of what might have been. My ache, spring green bursting,

scalpel sharp, sings of loss and love. And words unsaid,
gain power rolling round, a litany of stones
on a riverbed of tears waiting for a voice to be heard.
By what measure do we mark
our steps of abandonment? How far is too far
for a safe return? We should have had heart,
to name the path we walked,
to talk, to speak of mystery.
Yet we remain bound in silence,
out of touch, at a distance.
Here I am, looking for words,
fuelled by memories
and I burn with love
Pages of a life, shared, longed for still,
this is the song I sing now.
And therein lies the deeper truth.
This too will pass

Coming ready or not.

Snow

White falling upon the earth
 a lovers touch
carving paths to the heart

Temple woman

An arthritic day, no strength
left in its closing grip.
A bloom no longer, the colours
bleached and a scent of dust,
whispering petals in sand.
Like water in cupped hands
full of fingered cracks,
all gone, all gone.
A parchment of skin,
creased tight around years,
worn thin as a fashion gown.
And in the withering lies the seed,
the sacramental offering,
gladly given.
Done. All done.

The passing of a prodigal son

An old man shuffling.
Life lines scratched in fallen sand,
shifting.
The withered touch
dustlike upon the breath,
dry as dust,
and the falling whispers
of the coming apart of the sand,
and the falling whispers
of the last gasp crumpling,
and the falling whispers
of the lovers return.

Evening Rain

Still in its falling,
the weeping sigh of tears
without breath to beat
battering softly;
a panting sob of sepia whispers
kissing gently naked a dying day,
autumn leaves and other memories
unkempt with passion.
And in its grief still falling.

Printed in Poland
by Amazon Fulfillment
Poland Sp. z o.o., Wrocław

62770672R00038